MW01632764

MUNÍRIH KHÁNUM
Memoirs and Letters

MUNÍRIH KHÁNUM
the wife of ‘Abdu’l-Bahá.

MUNÍRIH KHÁNUM
Memoirs and Letters

by Munírih Khánum

translated by
Sammireh Anwar Smith

KALIMÁT PRESS
LOS ANGELES

Manufactured in the United States of America.

Library of Congress Cataloguing-in-Publication Data

Munírih, Khánum, 1847-1938.
Munírih Khánum: memoirs and letters.

Includes bibliographies.
1. Munírih, Khánum, 1847-1938. 2. Baha'i Faith—Biography. 3. 'Abdu'l-Bahá, 1844-1921—Family—Biography. I. Smith, Sammireh Anwar. II. Title.
BP395.M6A3 1987 297'.89'0924 [B] 86-34262
ISBN 0-933770-51-0

Kalimát Press
1600 Sawtelle Boulevard, Suite 34, Los Angeles, California 90025

Cover design by Rick Kjarsgaard.

Translator's Dedication

To my mother, Monireh Anvar,
and my daughter, Corinne Munírih

Contents

Translator's Note

Munírih Khánum remains a relatively unknown figure in Bahá'í history. This book will perhaps serve to make her more widely known within the English-speaking world.

In the first section, we are presented with some memories of her early life. These include anecdotes from her father, Mírzá Muḥammad-'Alí Nahrí, also from her uncle, Áqá Mírzá Hádí, and from Khadíjih Bigum, the widow of the Báb. Unfortunately, her account ends with her marriage to 'Abdu'l-Bahá in 1871. Of the fifty years or so of that marriage she provides us with no account.

We do not know when these memories were written, but some two years after 'Abdu'l-Bahá's passing in 1921, a copy was sent by Munírih Khánum and Shoghi Effendi to Ahmad Sohrab in America for translation into English. Sohrab's translation appeared early in 1924. At that time of sorrow, this precious memoir of the Holy Family was a sweet balm. Unfortunately, Sohrab's translation is far from ideal. He interpreted the text rather freely, and he omitted many lines. Hence the need for a new translation.

The second section of the book consists of a series of letters written in the aftermath of 'Abdul-Bahá's passing. "Caught in the talons of the eagle of sorrow," Munírih Khánum gives voice to her lament at her separation from her beloved. Later letters turn to more practical matters: the education of girls, and the service of women to the Cause of God. There is also a lament at the passing of Bahíyyih Khánum, 'Abdu'l-Bahá's sister. The letters have not been published together in English before, although translations of some have appeared in issues of *Star of the West*.

Some readers may find the style she uses to express the intensity of her sorrow excessive. But in this Munírih Khánum reflects the writing style of the late Qájár period, when everything was written in extremes and superlatives.

I would like to express my thanks to Lily Ayman for her time and patience in answering my many questions; to Frank Mausley, Moojan Momen, and Peter Smith for reading the translation, offering their suggestions, and smoothing out any mistakes; and to Anthony A. Lee for his editorial advice and encouragement.

Sammireh A. Smith
Bangkok
November 1986

Foreword

Because the early history of the Bahá'í Faith is set in Iran, a male-dominated society, the information that has been handed down to us by the early Bábí and Bahá'í historians—themselves conditioned to a great extent by the society around them—tends to concentrate on the men of that history. The women are assigned a subordinate, background role. With the exception of such outstanding figures as Ṭáhirih, few details are given of what the women were thinking or doing. And yet, we can be fairly certain that the role of women was important.

During the Bábí period, we know that but for the support of the women, it would not have been possible for the Bábís of Nayríz and Zanján to hold out against the royal troops. One European who visited Zanján during the Bábí upheaval commented: "They [the Bábís] fight in the most obstinate and spirited manner, the women even, of whom several have been killed, engaging in the strife."[1] Of the Nayríz upheaval, Nabíl records: "The uproar caused by their [the Bábís'] womenfolk, their amazing audacity and self-confidence, utterly demoralised their opponents and paralysed their efforts."[2] During the ministry of Bahá'u'lláh, the period with which this book is principally concerned, a number of individual women gained distinction through their teaching efforts and their heroism.

We know that the writings of Bahá'u'lláh contain passages that speak of the equality of men and women. It is also certain that the Bahá'ís in Iran, during the ministry of Bahá'u'lláh, both perceived themselves and were perceived by others as being a community that tended toward the elevation of the status of women. A Bahá'í in Isfahan said to E. G. Browne in 1887: "We are recommended to take to ourselves only one wife, to treat our families with tenderness and gentleness . . . we believe that women ought to be allowed to mix freely with men, and should not be compelled to wear the veil."[3] Curzon, who almost certainly did not obtain his information directly from Bahá'ís, reflected the manner in which Bahá'ís were perceived by the general population of Iran, which he visited in 1889: "The Bab and Beha in their writings have enjoined the disuse of the veil, the abolition of divorce, polygamy and concubinage, in other words of the harem, and greater liberty of action for the female sex."[4]

What we are less certain about, however, is how the Bahá'í women of this period saw themselves; how they viewed their role within the Faith; and what they perceived to be the impact of the Faith on a woman's life and on her rights. Nor can we be certain of what those women who were not Bahá'ís thought of the Faith; how they were influenced by it; or to what extent the Bahá'í religion may have promoted the gradual rise of the later movement to ameliorate the position of women in Iranian society.

One of the most important documents that can at least shed some light on these questions is the present narrative. It is an autobiographical sketch written by one of the eminent Bahá'í women of this period, Munírih Khánum, the wife of 'Abdu'l-Bahá.

Munírih Khánum was born into one of the most distinguished families of Isfahan. Her father, a descendant of the Prophet Muḥammad, and her mother were both children of wealthy merchants. They were closely connected by marriage to Sayyid Muḥammad Báqir Shaftí, who in his day had been the most powerful and influential cleric in Iran. They were also connected with another important family of ulama, the Khátúnábádís, among whom the position of Imám-Jum'ih of Isfahan had become hereditary. Thus, when this family became Bábís, and later Bahá'ís, they were in the anomalous and precarious position of being so in the midst of some of the most important ulama of the city.

From her childhood, Munírih Khánum was involved in some of the major events of Bábí and Bahá'í history. Her father, Mírzá Muḥammad-'Alí, had been a Shaykhí and had become a Bábí shortly after the Declaration of the Báb. He met the Báb in Isfahan and later participated in the conference of Badasht. Munírih Khánum herself grew up during the critical period when the Bábí community was being transformed into the Bahá'í community. Isfahan, where she lived, was one of the most important Bahá'í communities in Iran and her family was in many ways the pivot of that community.

Then later, in 1871, Bahá'u'lláh gave instructions for Munírih Khánum to be brought to 'Akká, where she was married to 'Abdu'l-Bahá. From that time onward, Munírih Khánum was, of course, closely connected with the central events of Bahá'í history until her death in 1938. But this narrative deals principally with the period of her life in Iran.

Women in nineteenth-century Iran were regarded as being much inferior to men, both in regard to their intellectual capacity and their spiritual worth. The religiously devout men looked on them with suspicion and disdain as a potential cause of the loss of their religious purity; women were regarded as having been placed on earth to lead men astray. The less religious would merely think of women as a source of sexual pleasure and domestic management. They were not much above chattels and slaves, certainly not worthy of being consulted about family affairs or entrusted with making any decisions for themselves. Indeed, a woman's temperament was felt to be totally unsuitable for any serious deliberation or rational thought.

As a result, few women received any education, and

there were almost no opportunities to make any meaningful contribution to society outside of domestic commitments. A woman's social contacts were limited to her own husband, her immediate male relatives, and a circle of other women. She was strictly and jealously guarded from contacts with other men. She might be killed by her husband with impunity on the mere suspicion of infidelity. Although Islam granted women certain strictly defined rights, few of them were able to exercise these rights, since there was no mechanism whereby they could act in society independently of men. Nor did wealth lead to any improvement in a woman's lot; the women of the upper classes were caged in the vacuous monotony of harem life. Thus for most women, the only way to exert any influence over their own lives was to dominate their husbands by teasing, cajoling, and intriguing. Many women achieved a degree of power in this way—but this provoked more distrust and disdain on the part of men and, not suprisingly, often led to divorce.

Although the teachings of Bahá'u'lláh had elevated the status of women, there were severe limitations on the extent that this could be put into practice in the Bahá'í community of Iran because of the prevailing social situation. Although the Bahá'í community led the way with regard to women's emancipation, the majority of Bahá'ís at this time were recent converts and were still much under the influence of the society around them and of their former ways of thinking. Moreover, the severe persecutions that occurred frequently put a brake on the extent to which reforms in the position of women could be introduced. Nevertheless, the Bahá'í community in Iran made strides in this direction and was to pioneer, in later generations, the introduction of education for women; the election of women to their representative bodies, the Local and National Spiritual Assemblies; and the encouragement of women to lead more active and fulfilled lives.

In this autobiographical narrative, we can catch a glimpse of what it was like to be a Bahá'í woman in those early days of the Faith. We can perceive something of women's aspirations and the frustrations inherent in their position. We can see that, far from being passive participants in events, Bahá'í women were actively engaged in teaching; we even have, in this narrative, a unique picture of an early "fireside" at which Munírih Khánum taught the Faith to the wife of Ḥájí Sayyid 'Alí, the uncle of the Báb. We also have some valuable reminiscences of another of the great female figures of the Faith, the wife of the Báb, whom Munírih Khánum met on her way to 'Akká. Two other heroines enter Munírih Khánum's story briefly: Ṭáhirih, with whom her father and uncle were closely associated, and Shamsu'ḍ-Ḍuḥá, the wife of her uncle.[5]

This narrative is then one of the important sources for the history of the Bahá'í Faith. Our only regret must be that Munírih Kh́ánum did not write at greater length of her experiences.

Moojan Momen
Cambridge, England

Notes

1. Abbot to Shiel, 30 Aug. 1850, FO 60 153, quoted in Momen, *Bábí and Bahá'í Religions* (Oxford, 1981) p. 118.

2. *The Dawn-Breakers, Nabíl's Narrative*, trans. by Shoghi Effendi, U.S. Ed. (Wilmette, Ill., 1936) p. 487; British Ed. (London, 1953) pp. 359–60.

3. *A Year Amongst the Persians*, New ed. (Cambridge, 1926) p. 235–6.

4. *Persia and the Persian Question* (London, 1892) vol. 1, p. 502.

5. See 'Abdu'l-Bahá, *Memorials of the Faithful*, trans. by Marzieh Gail (Wilmette, 1971) pp. 175–190, for an account of this lady.

MUNÍRIH KHÁNUM
The Memoirs

Bahá'í World Center

MUNÍRIH KHÁNUM

the wife of 'Abdu'l-Bahá, apparently taken while she was pregnant.

At the insistence of the handmaidens of God in America, and at the request of my spiritual sisters, I have written a brief account of the early years of my life and of my journey to the Holy Land.

In His Name, the Glory of the Most Glorious!

O Divine Providence! Thou seest and art a witness that all my limbs, my members, my heart, my soul, and my conscience bear testimony to the inexhaustible bounties which Thou has showered upon this unworthy handmaiden at Thy Threshold from the beginning of her life.

Should I attempt to give a full account of my life from the earliest days of my childhood, it would consist of wonders upon wonders. Indeed, I would be incapable of giving adequate thanks, and I would fall far short of a full description.

In truth, from the age of twelve until I stood in the Most Holy Presence, I had many dreams which are worth hearing—which can make one heedful, so that when one is subjected to difficulties and trials he may be able to bear them patiently. He will know that there is a wisdom hidden behind the mystic veil, and he will not become sorrow-stricken or dejected. Thus has the Ancient Tongue, the Greatest Name [Bahá'u'lláh], revealed in the Seven Valleys: "*If thou seest an injustice, behold in it Justice, and if thou dost experience unkindness, perceive it as kindness.*"*

Now, let me return to the story and relate past events. Even though I cannot remember all the events fully and have more or less forgotten many of them, yet at the insistence of some of the friends, a few pages will be written. Before starting, I would like to give an account of my family, in order to inform the reader.

My father was Mírza Muḥammad-'Alí Nahrí, the son of Ḥájí Sayyid Mihdí Nahrí, the son of Ḥájí Sayyid Muḥammad Hindí. Ḥájí Sayyid Muḥammad was born and raised in the village of Zavárih, near Isfahan. Having reached the age of maturity, he traveled to India. As he was descended from the pure and goodly seed of the Prophet,† a princess of a ruling Indian family accepted to marry him, in order to be privileged and honored by a relationship with the family of the Prophet. So it was that he sojourned in India and came to be known as

*Cf. *The Seven Valleys and the Four Valleys* (Wilmette, Ill., Rev. Ed., 1952) pp. 12–13.

†Muḥammad.

''Hindí,'' the Indian. This union gained him a vast fortune and he lived in the grand style of a member of the royal family.

After some time he became the father of two sons. His first son was Ḥájí Sayyid Mihdí, who became the sole inheritor of his father's fortune. This son left India for the holy city of Najaf and took up residence there, establishing farms, houses, caravanserais, shops, and other such properties in Karbala and Najaf. Of his inheritance, he spent a third on building a waterway in Najaf. Thus he became known by the title ''Nahrí.''* This title has been handed down through the family, and to this day his descendants are known by it.

Ḥájí Sayyid Mihdí Nahrí had several children, both male and female. One of them was my father Áqá Mírzá Muḥammad-'Alí Nahrí; and another was my uncle Áqá Mírzá Hádí, the father-in-law of the King of Martyrs,† upon him be innumerable greetings and praise!

There is a story connected to the above which I will tell: While Ḥájí Sayyid Muḥammad was living in India, a well-known and celebrated astrologer, unique in that age, drew up his horoscope. The astrologer forecast that

*The name is derived from *nahr* (river).

†Mírzá Muḥammad-Ḥasan of Isfahan was titled the King of Martyrs by Bahá'u'lláh after he and his brother, Mírzá Muḥammad-Ḥusayn, titled the Beloved of Martyrs, were killed for the Faith in 1879.

from among his children and grandchildren a number would be living at the time of the appearance of the Promised Qá'im, and they would become whole-hearted devotees of His Cause.

As the Ḥájí had complete confidence in the judgment of the astrologer, he accepted this prediction as certain and firm. In his will, he included the following in his own hand: "After my specific bequests are distributed among my heirs, all that remains in cash and other effects must be preserved and then presented to the Promised One, may His praise be glorified." Leaving this will behind, he bade farewell to this world and hastened on to merciful Providence.

When the call of the new Revelation was raised from Shiraz, my father and uncle started out for that city without even returning to their homes or informing their families. Both of them hastened to the presence of the Beloved. The other brothers, who were engrossed in worldly affairs and who were deprived of righteousness and the worship of truth, seized this opportunity and, conspiring with the ulama of Najaf and Karbala, accused the two brothers, Mírzá Muḥammad-'Alí and Mírzá Hádí, of being infidels with no rights to their inheritance. They exposed them as Bábís and seized all their wealth and possessions, paying no heed whatsoever to their father's will.

When my father and uncle discovered what their brothers had done, they turned their backs completely on the world and its inhabitants and closed their eyes on their father's wealth. From then on they strived day and night to sacrifice themselves in the Path of Truth. They had in their possession a small treasure chest from their father, which according to their father's will and his wishes they presented to Ṭáhirih,* may God exalt her station. During the days Ṭáhirih was in Baghdad and Karbala, she defrayed the expenses of her journeys from the contents of this chest. May the two brothers be blessed for their pure intentions.

If I were to attempt a description of the time Ṭáhirih spent with my father and uncle and their families, and the fervor of those days, this piece would be lengthened greatly. If I find an opportunity in the future, then I will write a brief account of those circumstances.

Now I would like to give a description of my grandmother, that is, my father's mother. She was an extremely devout and pure woman. One night in a dream, she saw two full moons rise out of the well of her house and nest within her bosom. The intensity of her excitement, joy, and bewilderment woke her from her sleep. Before sunrise, she went joyously to the house of Ḥájí Sayyid Muḥammad Báqir, an important personage, a *mujtahid* whose word was undisputed and whose com-

*Also known as Qurratu'l-'Ayn. She was one of the chief disciples of the Báb, a Letter of the Living, and the only woman to be so named.

mands were binding upon all in Persia. Indeed, he had no peer or equal in his lifetime. My grandmother related her dream to him and asked him to interpret it. He said to her, "Be happy. Be of good cheer! For God will bless you with two children, who will illumine and enlighten your family like two bright moons."

At about that time it became obvious that my grandmother was pregnant. At the appointed time my father, Mírzá Muḥammad 'Alí, was born and was followed a year and three months later by my uncle, Mírzá Hádí. When the two brothers reached the age of maturity, my father became eager to study the arts and sciences. He entered the seminary of Kásihgarán and pursued his studies. My uncle, on the other hand, followed the mystic path of seclusion, living in retirement and practicing piety and contemplation. He became a trusted confidant of the ulama. It was for this latter reason that the previously mentioned mujtahid, Sayyid Muḥammad Báqir gave his niece, later titled Shamsu'ḍ-Ḍuḥá,* in marriage to my uncle. They took up residence in Isfahan.

When my father finished his education in the seminary, he set out for the Holy Shrines.† In Karbala he joined the circle of Ḥájí Sayyid Káẓim Rashtí's students. There he became completely devoted to the Twin Lumi-

*See Foreword, note 5.

†The tombs of the Imám 'Alí and the Imám Ḥusayn, in the cities of Najaf and Karbala in Iraq.

Bahá'í World Center

MÍRZÁ MUḤAMMAD-ḤASAN
titled the King of Martyrs.

naries,* who remain brilliant stars unequalled in the sphere of existence. After a while, my father married.

My uncle, Mírzá Hádí, also came to Karbala with his family. There he associated with my father and with the Shaykhís, until the year 1260 A.H. (1844 A.D.) when they heard the Call of the Promised One by the name of the Báb, from Shiraz. As soon as they heard this message, they hastened from Karbala for Shiraz, without informing the members of their households.

The reason for their haste was to ascertain for themselves the truth of the person who had raised this Call. Because when they had attended Ḥájí Sayyid Káẓim Rashtí's classes, they had repeatedly seen His Holiness the Báb and had observed remarkable signs and manners apparent in His holy Person. In connection with this, my uncle used to relate the following:

> Before the year sixty,† when Ḥájí Sayyid Káẓim Rashtí was in Karbala, occupied in guiding and teaching people, and proclaiming that "the Kingdom of God is at hand," my brother and I were among his students, many of whom had been students of the late Shaykh Aḥmad Aḥsá'í. We attended the classes every day. One day we went on pilgrimage to the Shrine of the Lord of the Martyrs,‡ upon

*Shaykh Aḥmad al-Aḥsá-í and his successor, Sayyid Káẓim Rashtí, the leaders of the Shaykhí school.

†1260 A.H. or 1844 A.D.

‡Imám Ḥusayn, the martyred grandson of the Prophet Muḥammad.

Bahá'í World Center

MÍRZÁ MUḤAMMAD-ḤUSAYN
titled the Beloved of Martyrs.

him be greetings and praise. We passed over the sacred threshold and saw a young sayyid possessed of the utmost beauty, comeliness, serenity, and dignity. He stood before the Shrine with the greatest humility and respect, praying and chanting. When I saw such dignity and observed His perfection and beauty, I was so overcome that I was transfixed, in a state of utter bewilderment.

Every day I had heard from Sayyid Káẓim that the advent of the Promised One was at hand, that all must constantly be seeking Him and inquiring about Him—for the Lord of Revelation was present among men and associating with them, but the people were veiled from Him and heedless of His presence. I said to myself: Praise be to God! Maybe He is the hidden Qá'im come on pilgrimage to the Shrine of His Ancestor.

I sat where I was, listened to His melodious chanting and observed His behavior. Tears flowed from His eyes like vernal showers. He finished His pilgrimage without entering the inner enclosure and left in a state of utmost humility. Much perplexed, I said: O Lord, who is this holy Personage? I followed Him until He entered a house. I then enquired about the identity of the residents of that house from the neighbors. They replied that they were sayyids and Shirazi merchants who had been there for only a few days. So I knew that that Great One was from Shiraz.

From then on I would encounter Him every day at the Shrine. During the days of His seclusion in Karbala, He often illumined Sayyid Káẓim's classes with the light of His Beauty. Whenever He entered the class, the greatest respect and honor would be shown to Him by the sayyid.

After some time He left for Bushihr and Shiraz, and Sayyid Káẓim passed away.*

My brother and I were in Karbala when the call of the Revelation called "Babism" was raised from Shiraz. As soon as I heard it, my heart immediately turned to that holy Being, and His smiling countenance appeared before me. I said to my brother: "My dear brother, I swear to God, that the Lord of this Call must be that same young sayyid of Shiraz who occasionally attended the classes of the late Sayyid Káẓim."

And so, my brother and I set out for Shiraz with great speed. But on the way we heard that the Báb had gone to Mecca, so I returned to Karbala. My brother headed for Isfahan in order to meet the Bábul-Báb.†

This was my uncle's story as repeatedly related by his wife Shamsu'ḍ-Ḍuhá.

Now, on his return to Isfahan my father took a room in that same seminary of Kásihgarán. His wife was still residing in Karbala. He stayed there until the Bábul-Báb went from Shiraz to Isfahan to proclaim the Faith publicly at the command of the Primal Point,‡ may my life be a sacrifice to Him. In this way he guided many souls to the new Cause: among them was my father, who was

*On December 31, 1843.

†Mullá Ḥusayn Bushrú'í, titled the "Gate of the Gate" by the Báb Himself.

‡The Báb.

led to the path of knowledge and faith. Soon after this, he received the news that his wife had passed away.

At that time there was a well-known merchant in Isfahan Ḥájí Áqá Muḥammad* who was one of the new believers. He was devoted to my father, and one day he said to him: "Since your wife has passed away and you have no children, it would be better for you to leave the seminary and this secluded life and come live with us. I have a sister whom I would like to give in marriage to you whenever it is agreeable to you, so that the bonds of love and affection may thus be strengthened and made permanent between us."

My father readily consented to this suggestion. Ḥájí Áqá Muḥammad consulted his mother about the matter, and she not only had no objections, but was eager to bring about the union. She said, "Last night in a dream I saw a sayyid with a radiant face come to our house carrying two lamps. That sayyid is this very man, and you must hasten the whole business."

Therefore, Ḥájí Áqá Muḥammad prepared a betrothal feast, and his sister, who became my mother, was promised to him. My father had no children from his first marriage, and after being married to his second wife for two years they still had no children. This continued until the time when the Báb came from Shiraz to Isfa-

*Ḥájí Áqá Muḥammad Naqshínih-Furúsh.

han* and was a guest in the house of the Imám Jum'ih.† My uncle, Áqá Mírzá Ibráhím, the father of those twin shining lights the Beloved of Martyrs and the King of the Martyrs, was appointed by the Imám Jum'ih to be the Báb's host, and was privileged and honored to serve Him. One night the Báb accepted my uncle's invitation to dinner, and his house was blessed by His holy Presence. The following were present at that dinner:

Mírzá Sayyid Muḥammad, the Imám Jum'ih

Mír Muḥammad Ḥusayn, the brother of the Imám who later was instrumental in the martyrdom of the Beloved of Martyrs and the King of Martyrs. The Supreme Pen [of Bahá'u'lláh] gave him the title "She-serpent" (*raqshá'*).

Áqá Sayyid Muḥammad Riḍáy-i Pá Qal'i'i

Ḥájí Áqá Muḥammad-i Naqshínih-Furúsh, my mother's brother

Mírzá Ibráhim Táj

Mullá Muḥammad Taqí Hirátí, the father of Áqá Mírzá Muḥammad-'Alí,‡

Áqá Mírzá Ibráhím, my uncle and the owner of the house.

*In 1846.

†The cleric who leads the Friday prayers in the main mosque of the city.

‡Áqá Mírzá Muḥammad-'Alí became a Bábí during the Báb's stay in Isfahan. He was a relative of the Imám Jum'ih.

Those present at that feast received the bounties and favors of the Báb until food was served, and all partook of both a material and a spiritual feast. During supper, the Báb turned to one of those present and asked after my father's children. That person replied that my father had married twice but had no children. His Holiness offered a spoonful of His sweet to my father. He ate it, and as he did so it passed through his mind that it must be the wish of the Báb for him to have children.

When the meal was over my father told my mother all that had passed, and she, too, ate a little of the Báb's sweet. After that night, it became apparent that she was pregnant.

I was born eight months and nine days later. After three years Ḥájí Sayyid Yaḥyá was born, and after another three years my sister Ráḍiyyih Bagum. Five years later, my other sister Guhar Bagum was born. Thus they had three daughters and one son.

The Báb was taken from Isfahan to Tabriz and Mákú.* An order was received from Him instructing all the believers to gather under the black standard which was being raised in Khurasan.† My father prepared for the journey, and before he left he told my brother (who

*In 1847.

†Shí'í Muslim tradition held that the army of the Qá'im would come from Khurasan, under a black flag, to conquer the world.

was expecting me): "I am setting out on a journey. I do not know what the outcome of it will be. Perhaps I will be martyred. So my instruction to you is that if God gives us a child, you should call it 'Alí if it is a boy; and if a girl, then call her Fátimih." This was my father's will as spoken to my mother. He then set out for Khurasan with a group of about twenty-five men. At that time,* the Blessed Beauty [Bahá'u'lláh] was at Badasht with Quddús and Ṭáhirih. Every day the believers would gather there from the surrounding areas, until the Badasht conference was over. Then the Army of God set out for Khurasan.

It was then that the incidents of Niyálá and the stoning of the believers took place. These events at Niyálá have been recorded at length in books covering the history of the period.† My uncle received severe injuries and died on the way. My father gave the following account of the episode:

> When the believers dispersed from Niyálá in groups, each taking a different route, the inhabitants of Niyálá followed them and martyred whoever they could lay their hands on. My brother and I and several other people continued on our way [after the attack], when suddenly my brother was

*1848.

†See, for instance, *The Dawn-Breakers. Nabíl's Narrative* (Wilmette, Ill., 1932) pp. 298–300.

overcome with a feeling of great weakness. We arrived at a ruined caravanserai, and here we spent the night. My brother died there, and the other friends, fearing attack by our enemies, each crept away in some direction during the night. So, only I and my brother's corpse remained. In the morning, I left the caravanserai and stood bewildered and confused at the roadside, wondering how to go about burying my brother and how to save my own skin from the enemies.

Suddenly, I saw a woman coming toward me from a distance. When she reached me she asked: "Who are you and why are you standing here?"

I told her: "My brother died in this caravanserai last night, and I am at a loss as to how to go about burying him."

The woman said, "Do not worry about this, for I have come to perform this very service. Last night I dreamt that her holiness Fátimih Zahra,* upon her be peace, said to me, 'One of my children has died in this caravanserai. You must go tomorrow and bury him.' Now, I have come to fulfil her command."

She said this and hurried back to her village. She returned a few minutes later with the gravediggers and all that was necessary for a funeral. My brother's body was washed in a stream of water, a shroud was wrapped around

*The revered daughter of the Prophet Muḥammad and wife of the Imám 'Alí. Shí'í Muslims regard her as the holiest woman in Islam.

> him, and, as he had requested that he be buried by the highway which pilgrims take on their way to Karbala, he was buried right there. The villagers then returned to their homes and I turned toward Tehran.
>
> From there I continued to Isfahan in a state of utter exhaustion, having been stoned and badly injured, with my brother dead and the whereabouts of my sister, who was with Ṭáhirih, unknown. In such a condition I entered Isfahan at a time when it was impossible for anyone even to mention the word "Bábí."

In spite of all these calamities, my father taught the new Faith day and night to such an extent that his elder brother, the father of the King of the Martyrs and the Beloved of Martyrs [Áqá Mírzá Ibráhím] sent him a message saying: "My dear brother, you Bábís seem to have such a commotion in your heads that it prevents you from recognizing any danger or calamity. If this is true, then you should leave this quarter of the city. My life is in danger. I will lose my children and my possessions because of your actions."

My father replied with the following message: "I will not sell my faith for worldly considerations. I have relinquished my claim to my father's limitless wealth, and as long as there is breath in my body I will endeavor to proclaim this message."

After this, he bought a house in the S͟háh S͟háhán quarter of the city and spent all his time with Zaynu'l-

Muqarrabín and Sayyid Ismá'íl Dhabíh, who later committed suicide in Baghdad.* Together they taught the Faith, and among those who accepted the Faith at that time were the twin shining lights, the Beloved of Martyrs and the King of Martyrs.

Soon after my father and the two brothers set out together to attain the Holy Presence [of Bahá'u'lláh] in Baghdad. I heard the following from the two brothers many times:

> On the way I told my uncle†: When we are in His Presence, you must be our voice and the interpreter of our hearts."
>
> My uncle would reply: "Rest assured, for in Badasht I was very close to Him."
>
> We entered Baghdad, and at the hour of meeting Bahá'u'lláh, my uncle—who had claimed such intimate friendship—was struck dumb. He was so humbled that he did not have the courage to utter a single word. No matter how much the Ancient Beauty would bestow His favors, my uncle just became more silent and self-effacing, until His Holiness said, "Jináb-i Mírzá Muḥammad-'Alí, you and I were friends and fellow-travelers at Badasht." We were then permitted to leave.

*Zaynu'l-Muqarrabín later became an Apostle of Bahá'u'lláh. Regarding, Sayyid Ismá'íl Dhabíh, see *God Passes By* (Wilmette, Ill., 1944) pp. 136–37.

†That is, Munírih Khánum's father.

Bahá'í World Center

A VIEW OF BAGHDAD
showing the Tigris River.

I turned to my uncle and said, "Uncle, what overcame you?"

He replied: "I swear by God, the One, the Single, that He is not the same Jináb-i Bahá whom this servant met at Badasht. Nay, rather, with absolute confidence and assurance my heart bears witness that He is the Promised One of the Bayán, He whom God will make manifest." Our uncle was one of those who became a believer in the Ancient Beauty before His declaration.

I was eleven years old when my father returned from Baghdad, and I heard him tell my mother several times: "It is my intention to take Fátimih to the Blessed Household." Then, I would say to myself: O God, where is this Blessed Household? Karbala has its own name, so where is this place?

Soon after, my father passed away. Responsibility for our affairs passed into the hands of relatives on both my father's and my mother's side. Everyone was extremely kind to me and looked upon me as a gift granted on the night the Báb came to the feast. Because of their affection toward me, whoever they considered good and suitable they would chose as my future husband. For this reason, these two important families were constantly competing and arguing. This matter caused so much bad feeling that I, at the beginning of my youth, lost all desire for any pleasure. I would often say: "I do not accept anyone. I will not consent to marry anyone, should he be Christ from heaven, or the Joseph of this age."

Instead, I spent my time praying and reading Tablets. I would recite the Long Obligatory Prayer daily and would keep both the fast of the Bayán and the Muslim fast. My heart did not incline toward worldly pleasures at all, to such an extent that—as God is my witness—I myself was bewildered and would wonder why I wished to keep away from these earthly matters. I would argue to myself that I loved my relatives and near ones greatly, so why did I not obey them and follow their advice?

Everyday at sunset, I would go onto the roof of the house to chant poetry and prayers until well into the evening. My mother would become vexed with me and would ask why I behaved in this way. Finally, one night I came down from the roof in a bad temper and found myself very depressed. That night I dreamed I was walking in a wilderness, and someone was following me. Suddenly he caught up with me, and I saw that he was riding a horse. He said, "Why are you afraid? Come, climb up behind me and I will take you wherever you want to go." He helped me mount and asked: "What is your desire?"

I said, "I beg God to give me two wings, so I can fly."

The rider took hold of me and held me up. Suddenly, I realized that I had two wings and was flying. I flew for some time until I reached a vast arena full of people. I saw a high pulpit on which the Prophet Muḥammad stood. All the prophets and messengers were seated there. At that moment, I turned into a dove. I flew up and settled in one of the niches on the pulpit.

The Prophet placed a necklace around my neck and I flew away to unseen places that no words can describe. There I saw people in a state of prayer, among them my mother. I gave her the necklace and flew away again.

Then, I awoke. I was exhilarated and began to cry. My poor mother came to me to find out what was wrong. All that I day I felt strange. After that, on most nights I would dream that I was soaring. And I was extremely happy because I knew that dreams of flying are good omens.

Days passed in this manner until the King of the Martyrs and the Beloved of the Martyrs insisted, backed up by the Imám Jum'ih, that I had to marry their younger brother. Resigning myself to their wishes, I accepted. This youth would bring all the news from Adrianople, from the Presence of the Beloved, to Isfahan. He was a most dignified, loving, pleasant, and attractive person; and all our relatives and friends were delighted.

Preparations for the wedding were made with the greatest care. The young man would send me letters full of love and happiness every day. A house was specially built for us, and all manner of means for our well-being and comfort were provided. The wedding night arrived and, according to Persian custom, all our friends and acquaintances accompanied us to the house of the bridegroom's uncle. With much kindness and amiability they sang and played and made merry until four in the morning. After four, my cousin welcomed me formally, and we were taken to the house built for us. The crowd then dispersed, except for a few close relatives who soon left the room also.

I saw that the young man was not speaking at all. He did not try to remove the veil from my face. He did not say: Are you a guest or my cousin or an acquaintance? Where were you?

I tolerated this for some hours and did not utter a single word. Then, I detected several people standing behind the lattice, waiting. I had no option but to say to him: "What is wrong with you that you say nothing?"

He replied: "I have such a headache that I cannot speak." And again he fell silent.

What can I say? No one had ever heard of such a situation. Nobody would believe it, except for the people of Isfahan who saw with their own eyes and heard with their own ears. His brothers and all the relatives became sad and depressed. They would not speak to him. And that poor soul was bewildered and dejected also. He swore that: "I am not responsible for this. I cannot approach her. I will submit to anything except intimacy with my cousin. There is surely a wisdom in this that will become apparent."

Life continued like this, with him remaining silent and confused. He spoke to no one and befriended none.

Then one night, we were alone in the house except for a maidservant. She saw his head bowed down onto his lap, and after a while she approached him and saw that he had yielded up his life. Upon him be the mercy of God, and His favor!

This story is related so that, if in the world of being difficulties and trials encompass a person, then he should know that behind the mystic veil there is a wisdom concealed. In reality, that youth was an escort who delivered me to my true goal and ultimate destination. He it was who joined this drop to the Most Mighty Ocean.

After this incident, I forsook the world and its people. I cut myself off from all earthly attachments. With a heart full of the love of God alone, I occupied myself in reading verses and scripture and associating with the believers.

At about that time, Sayyid Mihdí Dahijí came to Isfahan at the instruction of the Ancient Beauty to proclaim the Faith. All the believers came to meet him, to inquire about news from the Holy Land, and to question him about the Beloved. Among them was Shamsu'ḍ-Ḍuḥá, a relative of the King of the Martyrs and my aunt. She asked: "While you were in the holy Presence [of Bahá'u'lláh] did you ever hear Him speak of any girl He may have selected to marry the Master?"

Sayyid Mihdí Dahijí replied: "I heard nothing about that. However, one day when the Blessed Beauty was in the outer rooms of the house, as He paced about He said, "Áqá Sayyid Mihdí, last night I had a strange dream. I dreamt that the face of the beautiful girl in Tehran,* whose hand in marriage we have asked from our brother Mírzá Ḥasan for the Most Great Branch, gradually became darkened and indistinct. At the same time, another girl appeared with a luminous face and a luminous heart. I have chosen her for the Most Great Branch.' That is all I have heard."

When my aunt returned home and saw me she said, "I swear by the one true God, at the very moment when Áqá Sayyid Mihdí told this story, I felt that—without a shadow of a doubt—you are that girl! You will see!"

With tears in my eyes I said, "May God forgive me! How can I be worthy? I beg you not to say this again and not to mention it to anyone."

Not long after this, a Tablet arrived from the Holy Land in honor of the King of Martyrs. In it the Blessed Beauty said, "We have accounted you as one of our near ones and kindred." When my relative read this phrase, he immediately sent for all the members of the family and asked: "Have any of you sent a petition to the

*S͟hah-Bánú K͟hánum, the niece of Bahá'u'lláh, was intended to be 'Abdu'l-Bahá's wife. But her uncle and guardian, Mírzá Riḍá-Qulí, blocked the proposed marriage. See *Bahá'u'lláh: The King of Glory* (Oxford, 1980) pp. 342–44.

Blessed Beauty? What is this bounty? What are the glad tidings in this Tablet?''

We all replied that no one had written anything.

The King of the Martyrs said, ''In that case, this Tablet must not be spread among the believers until its meaning becomes apparent.''

Several months later, Shaykh Salman* arrived in Isfahan from the Holy Land and told the King of Martyrs: ''I carry glad tidings and untold bounties. Your cousin, the daughter of the late Mírzá Muḥammad-'Alí, is to accompany me to Mecca with the Muslim pilgrims going there, as though we too are making a pilgrimage to the Kaaba. You must make preparations for this journey until the usual time of Ḥájj, when we can set out and travel by way of Shiraz and Bushihr. However, do not give out this news until two or three days before our departure.''

The time of pilgrimage arrived, and we set out for Shiraz with my brother Sayyid Yaḥyá and a servant boy. On our arrival in Shiraz, we went to stay in a pleasant caravanserai. In the evening, the Afnáns† came and took us to the house of the uncle of the Báb, Ḥájí Mírzá Sayyid Muḥammad, where we stayed that night. That house

*Believer who for forty years carried Tablets and letters back and forth between Bahá'u'lláh and the Bahá'ís of Iran. See *Memorials of the Faithful* (Wilmette, Ill., 1971) pp. 13–16.

†The relatives of the Báb.

Bahá'í World Center

THE HOUSE OF THE BÁB IN SHIRAZ
the upper floor.

seemed so holy and radiant to me that I felt it was one of the mansions of paradise. There we eagerly met the women of the Afnán household. There is no need to explain what I felt and what a spiritual state I experienced.

The next morning the wife of the Báb,* may the souls of all be a sacrifice to Him, came to bid us welcome. She seemed like the Virgin Mary or Fátimih Zahrá. She invited us to stay in her house, and we accompanied her there. Her house was that of the older uncle of the Báb, Jináb-i Ḥájí Mírzá Sayyid 'Alí, who later became one of the Seven Martyrs of Tehran. This house is situated next to the one in which the Báb was born. When we arrived, we were taken to visit the house of the Báb. One of the rooms of the house was locked.† No one ever entered it. However, the door was opened, and we entered and had the honor of spending an hour there. Afterwards, the wife of the Báb said, "I have been expecting you. Áqá Mírzá Ḥasan had written me to say that a visitor would be arriving."

From there we returned to the house where she was living, the house of the uncle of the Báb. The wife of the uncle of the Báb was also present. I found her to be a holy and pure woman, pious and prayerful, but she was

*Khadíjih Bagum. See *Khadíjih Bagum: The Wife of the Báb* (Oxford, 1981).

†This is the room in which the Báb first declared His Mission to Mullá Ḥusayn.

Bahá'í World Center

AN INTERIOR LIVING ROOM
of the House of the Báb in Shiraz, once occupied by the Báb's wife,
Khadíjih Bagum.

not fully convinced about the truth of this Cause. She remarked: "What a commotion our Mírzá 'Alí-Muḥammad has caused in the world! So many important people have perished, and so much blood has been shed!"

I replied to her: "O revered lady, your Mírzá 'Alí-Muḥammad was the Qá'im of the House of Muḥammad and the Promised One of all the sacred books. In every age, when the divine Call was raised, this same commotion took place in the world and rivers of blood flowed. You read the Qur'an day and night and know that it states: '. . . And whenever the Messengers came with that which your souls desired not, you proudly rejected them, calling some liars and slaying others.'* And again 'O the misery of men! No Messenger comes to them but they laugh him to scorn.' "†

I read several more verses of the Qur'an to her, but she objected, saying: "None but God and those well-versed in knowledge know the meaning of the Qur'án."

I acceded to this, saying: "Very well, I accept your wishes and opinions. Now, let us put the Qur'an aside and turn to the Mathnaví‡ in which we read how the Pharoah treated Moses; what the Palestinians did to Jesus Christ; and what the people of Hijaz inflicted on

*Qur'an 2:81.

†Qur'an 36:29.

‡A classic epic of mystic poetry composed in the thirteenth century by Jalálu'd-Dín Rúmí.

Bahá'í World Center

COURTYARD OF THE HOUSE OF THE BÁB
in Shiraz.

the Prophet Muḥammad. Most of these events are related in the Mathnaví as well as many in history books."

We spent much time reading the Mathnaví together, and all the women of the Afnán household would join us. Those were pleasant days, the sweetness of which cannot be forgotten. I heard that after we left Shiraz, the lady accepted the Faith.

While I was there I said to the wife of the Báb: "We have talked enough of these other matters. I beg of you to tell us of your life, and of your meeting with the Báb, and of your marriage to Him."

She said:

> I cannot recall everything, but because of your request I will relate all that I remember. The Báb's father, Áqá Sayyid Muḥammad Riḍá, was my cousin.* He was engaged in a small amount of trade. We were three sisters. One night I dreamt that Fáṭimih Zahrá had come to our house to propose that one of us marry her son. My sister and I went forward with joy and delight to welcome her. She arose and kissed me on the forehead. In my dream, I understood that she had selected me. I awoke in the morning exhilarated, and yet modesty forbade me from telling my dream to anyone. On that very day at noon, the Báb's mother came to our house. My sister and I went to greet her in the same way we had done in my dream. She arose and kissed me on the forehead and held me in her arms, then she left. My older sister told me that she had come to ask for my hand,

*Apparently, this is incorrect. They were not cousins.

and I said, "O, how fortunate I am!" I related the dream I had had and said, "This dream has brought joy to my heart."

After a few days, the betrothal was discussed and gifts were sent for the engagement. The Báb and his uncle set out for Bushihr at this time to engage in some commerce.

After that dream, whenever I met the mother of the Báb I showed her the greatest respect and courtesy, even though she was my own aunt.

I cannot remember now how long the Báb's trip lasted. While He was in Bushihr I dreamt that it was our wedding night and that I was sitting in His presence. He was wearing a green cloak around which there was writing. Within those writings, verses from the Qur'an were inscribed. One of the verses was the *Áyatu'l-núr* [the Verse of Light],* and light emanated from His person. The intensity of my happiness at seeing Him in this state woke me up. After this dream, I felt assured that He was a great personage and a great love for Him filled my heart. Yet I could not confide these thoughts to anyone. He returned from Bushihr after some time, and His uncle arranged the wedding ceremony. So, the marriage took place.† And still I found myself completely detached from material things and my heart attracted only by Him. I could see by His behavior, His words, His tranquility, and dignity that He was a great person. But I never imagined that He was the Promised One, the Qá'im. He spent most of His time in prayer and

*Qur'an 24:35.
†In 1842.

supplication. In the evenings, as was customary among merchants, He would ask for His bundle of papers and His account book, yet I would observe that these were not His business records. I would occasionally ask: "What are these papers?" He would smile and reply: "These are account books on the people of the world." If an unexpected guest suddenly arrived, He would cover the papers with a cloth.

To be brief, all close friends and relatives such as uncles and aunts were convinced of His greatness and showed Him great respect. So it continued, until the evening of May 22, 1844. That was the night when the Bábu'l-Báb came to visit Him and acknowledged His mission.

What an extraordinary night that was! The Báb said to me: "Tonight we will entertain a dear guest." His whole being was ablaze. I was most eager to hear what He had to say, but He turned to me and told me: "It is better if you go and sleep." I did not wish to disobey Him, but I remained awake all night and could hear His blessed voice until the morning, conversing with the Bábu'l-Báb, chanting verses, and presenting proofs and arguments.

Every day, from then on, the Báb entertained an unknown guest and they would converse in the same way. Should I wish to relate fully the sufferings and trials He had to bear in those days, I could not bear to say them, and you would not be able to endure hearing them. But I will relate the incident of His capture briefly.

One night we were asleep.* Suddenly, the chief of police,

*September 23, 1846.

Bahá'í World Center

ROOM WHERE THE BÁB DECLARED HIS MISSION
to Mullá Ḥusayn, the Bábu'l-Báb, in Shiraz.

the accursed 'Abdu'l-Ḥamíd Khán, entered with his men through the roof of the house and seized the Báb, who was clad only in a thin robe. They took Him away without any explanation. I never saw Him again.

I cannot describe the terrible trials, ordeals, and difficulties that occurred after this. I did not see even one of His friends or followers after his arrest. The doors were shut on all sides, and communications were cut off completely. One day I saw that Shiraz was in turmoil.* The populace was in an uproar and I could hear the loud noises of bugles and trumpets. People were saying that the heads of the martyrs of Nayríz had been brought into the city. The next day, with the same tumult and violence, those captured at Nayríz were paraded through the city. How I longed to meet a relative of one of those prisoners, but it was impossible. Two of the captives came to our house in the guise of beggars, but no one dared speak to them.

But time passed and so did those events. Now you have come to visit us, and we can speak of any matter without fear.

The wife of the Báb asked me whether I would stay with her for some time and meet with the women of the Afnán household every day. Shaykh Salmán, who was the leader of our party, replied that it would not be possible for us to stay longer in that city. It was the order of the Blessed Beauty that we should travel with the pilgrims to Mecca. So it was. We bade farewell to the wife of the

*The year was 1850.

Báb and the other ladies with great sorrow, weeping and lamenting, and we set out for Bushihr.

Just before we left, the wife of the Báb said, "I wish for two things from the Ancient Beauty: first, that one of the Blessed Leaves be united to the family of the Primal Point [the Afnán family], so that these two blessed Trees might also be united outwardly*; second, I would like permission to visit Him." When I later attained the presence of Bahá'u'lláh and conveyed these two requests, He granted them immediately. He commanded her brother (that is, the father of Mírzá Muḥsin) to set out from Yazd and travel to Shiraz in order to transport the wife of the Báb [to the Holy Land] as if she were going on pilgrimage to Mecca.

But because of various difficulties, when the gentleman set out from Ashkhabad ('Ishqábád) he wrote to his sister, the wife of the Báb, saying, "I have left. God willing, the means for your journey will somehow be provided." When she received this message, she was so grief-sticken that she fell ill. Two days later she passed away from this world of pain. She was buried in Sháh Chiráq in Shiraz.† When the Ancient Beauty was informed of this terrible matter, He was so distressed that He immediately sent an order to Áqá Mírzá Sádiq in-

*The women of Bahá'u'lláh's household were referred to as "Leaves." Eventually, two of Bahá'u'lláh's granddaughters married relatives of the Báb, uniting the two families.

†Many other relatives of the Báb were also buried there.

structing him "to send the entire family of the King of the Martyrs from Isfahan to the Holy Land without the slightest hesitation or excuse." This was obeyed accordingly.*

Such was our stay in Shiraz and our acquaintance with the wife of the Báb.

After our arrival in Bushihr from Shiraz, one afternoon we went to a caravanserai. As I had never seen the sea before, I immediately climbed onto the roof and saw a vast and limitless ocean. I thought to myself: I must travel across this sea, from one world to another. Thoughts of my family and friends, and many memories of my mother came to mind. I could not stop the tears from flowing. I thought of the high status of my near ones, of their great numbers, of how they dealt with one another—with utmost love and harmony. Praise be to God! They have now all scattered and dispersed in His path. Among them are the twin shining lights who offered their pure lives in the path of the Friend and whose mention adorns every gathering.

Let us return to the matter at hand. I came down from the roof in an indescribable condition—submerged in a sea of happiness, but sorrowful at my separation from my family and friends and my sisters. That night I felt very

*After the death of the King of the Martyrs, Bahá'u'lláh asked the entire family to come to the Holy Land, where they would be under His protection.

strange. Still fully dressed and wearing my full veil, I put my head on my saddle-bag and fell asleep.

I dreamt that I was wandering in a vast wilderness. A pearl necklace that I was wearing suddenly broke and all the pearls fell to the ground. With a heavy heart, I started to pick them up. Then I suddenly saw that each pearl was growing until it became the size of an egg or even larger. Some had joined together. They sparkled and shone so much that they illuminated the wilderness. It was so beautiful and pleasing that the words of the Báb recorded in the Persian Bayán came to mind: "Endeavor ye, to present every unique and precious object to Him whom God shall make manifest." I told myself that it would be good to take these pearls and present them to the Blessed Beauty when I attained His presence. A container appeared, and I placed the pearls in it and lifted it onto my head.

In a loud voice I called "O Thou whom God shall make manifest! O Thou whom God shall make manifest!" After proceeding for some time, I saw that a branch had grown out of the middle of the container. It seemed to be guiding me to the Holy Land by alternately rising and prostrating. As it did so, a melodious voice could be heard coming from the branch, intoning, "Alláh-u-Akbar! Alláh-u-A'ẓam! Alláh-u-Abhá!" I joined in with this glorification and praise.

My moans and exclamations in my sleep were so loud that my brother, Sayyid Yaḥyá, awoke and roused me saying, "Sister, sister, what has happened to you that you moan and cry out so much?"

I told him of my dream, but I could not describe it adequately. Right then and there, I wrote down all that had occurred in my dream and sent it to my mother in Isfahan.

The next day, we embarked on an eighteen-day sea voyage to Jeddah. From there we traveled to Mecca and carried out our duties as pilgrims. There we met some of the believers who were returning from the Holy Land via Mecca. Among them was Sayyid 'Alí-Akbar, the nephew of Sayyid Mihdí Dahijí, and his wife. When they found out that we were on our way to the Holy Land, they tried with all their might to prevent us from going there. They explained: "It is not permissible for anyone to go to 'Akká these days. Because of recent events, some believers have been imprisoned and absolutely nobody is allowed to enter 'Akká."

This news disturbed us a great deal and we wondered what we should do. Shaykh Salmán assured us, "Your case differs from all others. Be confident and rest assured that we will enter the Holy Land, even if all the believers might be chained and imprisoned."

After carrying out the requirements of the Muslim pilgrimage, we returned to Jeddah. A message from Áqá Mírzá Áqá Ján, Khádimu'lláh, was awaiting us: "You are instructed to remain in Jeddah until all the pilgrims

National Bahá'í Archives, Wilmette, Illinois

A VIEW OF 'AKKÁ
from the sea shore.

return to their homelands. From there, you can then proceed to Alexandria where you should wait until you receive our telegram."

We remained in Jeddah as directed until the pilgrims dispersed. We then set out for Alexandria in the company of seventeen other Bahá'ís. We stayed there until a telegram arrived from the Most Holy Presence instructing all those present to disperse except for the four of us who were to go directly to 'Akká on an Austrian steamer. Furthermore, we were told to remain on board once we arrived at 'Akká until 'Abdu'l-Aḥad came to get us, then we could disembark. Our fellow travelers all left, and we set out for our intended goal.

The steamer entered the port of 'Akká half an hour before sunset. 'Abdu'l-Aḥad did not come. All the passengers disembarked, and the steamer's cargo was unloaded. But still he did not appear. We were anxiously on the look out for him. My brother said, "Sister, it seems that we will have to return."

I replied, "My brother, of course we will obey. In the *Lawḥ-i madinatu'l-riḍa* (Tablet of the City of Resignation) He states: "The paradise of resignation is better than the paradise of My presence."

Night fell and the gang plank was raised. We were completely hopeless. Shaykh Salmán bellowed out constantly. Suddenly, 'Abdu'l-Aḥad's voice reached us like the trumpet of heaven, or a revelation from the All-Merciful. He came to the steamer in a private boat, the

KHÁJIH ABBÚD
the owner of the house in which the Holy Family lived in 'Akká.

gang plank was lowered, and we descended into the boat. It was very dark, and nobody was on the landing when we arrived there except for Jináb-i Kalím* and Kh̲ájih ‘Abbúd, the owner of the house in which the Blessed Beauty lived. Later, the Greatest Holy Leaf told me that the Master, ‘Abdu’l-Bahá, had also come to the landing place at Bahá’u’lláh’s instruction, but I did not see Him.

Together with Jináb-i Kalím, we went to the Kh̲án-i Jurayní.† The next morning all the women of the Household came to visit us in Jináb-i Kalím’s house, and we accompanied them into the presence of the Blessed Beauty.

With what words can I describe that meeting? His first utterance to me was: “We have received you into this prison at a time when the prison door is closed to all the believers, so that the power of God may become clear and evident to all.”

For five months we remained in Jináb-i Kalím’s house. On some days we would attain His [Bahá’u’lláh’s] Presence and then return to our home. Whenever Jináb-i Kalím visited Bahá’u’lláh, he would return and convey His infinite bounties as well as some gift. One

*Usually known as Áqáy-i Kalím, or Mírzá Músá, the younger brother of Bahá’u’lláh who accompanied Him in His exiles.

†A caravanserai, also known as Kh̲án-i ‘Umdán.

Bahá'í World Center

CARAVANSARI IN 'AKKÁ

day he returned saying, "I have brought you a wonderful gift. You have been renamed Munírih (Luminous) by Him."

Instantly I remembered Bahá'u'lláh's dream related to us in Isfahan by Sayyid Mihdí Dahijí. The Blessed Beauty had said: "I dreamt that I saw the daughter of my brother Mírzá Ḥasan become sick. Her color changed, and she gradually became weaker and more faded until she left this world. Then another girl appeared whose face was luminous and whose heart was luminous. I have chosen her for the Most Great Branch."

We continued to live in the house of Jináb-i Kalím for five months because of a lack of housing. Finally, Khájih 'Abbúd questioned Jináb-i Kalím about this matter and asked why the marriage had been delayed. Jináb-i Kalím did not give him a clear answer, until 'Abbúd himself realized that the problem was the lack of a room. Khájih 'Abbúd then opened a room from his own house, which adjoined the private quarters of the holy Household. He furnished the room with the utmost simplicity and purity, and then went to the Blessed Beauty to request Him to accept this room as he had prepared it for the Master. His request was accepted, and the night of union—preferable to a hundred thousand years—drew near.

On that night, I wore a white dress given to me by the Greatest Holy Leaf, and which was more precious than all the silks and brocades of paradise. At about three hours after sunset on that night of power, the life-giving

THE HOUSE OF ABBÚD
where ‘Abdu’l-Bahá and Munírih Khánum were married.

Bahá'í World Center

ROOM IN THE HOUSE OF ABBÚD
where the Kitáb-i Aqdas was revealed.

voice of the incomparable Beloved could be heard from the Supreme Source. I was summoned to the presence of the Blessed Beauty, attended by Ḥaḍrat-i Khánum.*

The Ancient Beauty was seated under a mosquito net. He said, "You have come! You are welcome!" Then He addressed me thus: "O My Leaf and My Handmaiden! Verily, we chose thee and accept thee to serve my Most Great Branch, and this is by my grace, which is not equalled by all the treasures of earth and heaven." After bestowing numerous favors, He said, "How many were the girls in Baghdad and Adrianople, and in this Most Great Prison who hoped to attain to this bounty, and whose hopes were not fulfilled. You must be thankful for this most great bestowal and great favor." Then He dismissed me and bade me to withdraw "under the protection of God." After hearing these heavenly words and observing such divine bestowals, you can imagine how I felt and what a world was before my eyes.

> Said the heavens to the earth:
> "If the Resurrection thou hast never seen,
> then behold!"

After that blessed and happy hour, I entered that sheltering paradise, immersed in worlds of ardent desire,

*Ásíyih Khánum, the Most Exalted Leaf, the wife of Bahá'u'lláh and the mother of 'Abdu'l-Bahá.

THE HOUSE OF 'ABBÚD
The Upper Courtyard.

attraction, effacement, and absolute nothingness. How blessed and exalted was that time! How joyous that hour in that room! There I observed the Most Great Branch in utmost grace, bounty, and majesty. Only God knows what happened at that time. After an hour or so, the Master's mother, the wife of Áqáy-i Kalím, the wife of the landlord, and their daughters all entered the room. The mother of Mírzá Muḥammad 'Alí had brought Tablets used especially for celebrating holy days and festive occasions. She handed me the Tablet that begins: "The gates of paradise are opened and the celestial youth hath appeared"* and told me to recite it. Without further ceremony, I took it and intoned it in a loud and melodious voice. From then on, whenever the wife of Kh͟ájih 'Abbúd saw me she would say: "I shall never forget that night and that meeting; the sweetness of your voice still rings in my ears. No bride had ever chanted so at her own wedding!"

Such were the events that took place in the Holy Land, and on my journey there—and of the dream before I arrived there, as well as my meeting with the wife of the Báb. Should I wish to write an account of the fifty years spent in the Presence of the Beloved of the Worlds ['Abdu'l-Bahá], I would need fifty years to do so, the seas

**Lawḥ-i g͟hulámu'l-k͟huld* (Tablet of the Youth of Paradise). See *The Revelation of Bahá'u'lláh*, vol. 1, p. 213ff.

would have to turn to ink and the trees into pens. All I can do is supplicate at the Threshold of Oneness, and beseech Him not to deny me His favors and bounties in all His worlds.

O Lord, I ask of Thee that the end of all affairs will be filled with goodness, honor and happiness. O Lord of the Worlds and Most Merciful of the Merciful!

The handmaiden of
His Threshold,
Munírih

National Bahá'í Archives, Wilmette, Illinois

'ABDU'L-BAHÁ AS A YOUNG MAN
taken in Adrianople, 1868.

MUNÍRIH KHÁNUM
Letters

The following section consists of "Letters of Lament" written by Munírih Khánum on the anniversaries of the passing of her husband, 'Abdu'l-Bahá, and His sister, the Greatest Holy Leaf. Also included is a letter addressed to Bahá'í women concerning education, and a letter to the Bahá'í women of Tehran concerning the service of women to the Cause of God.

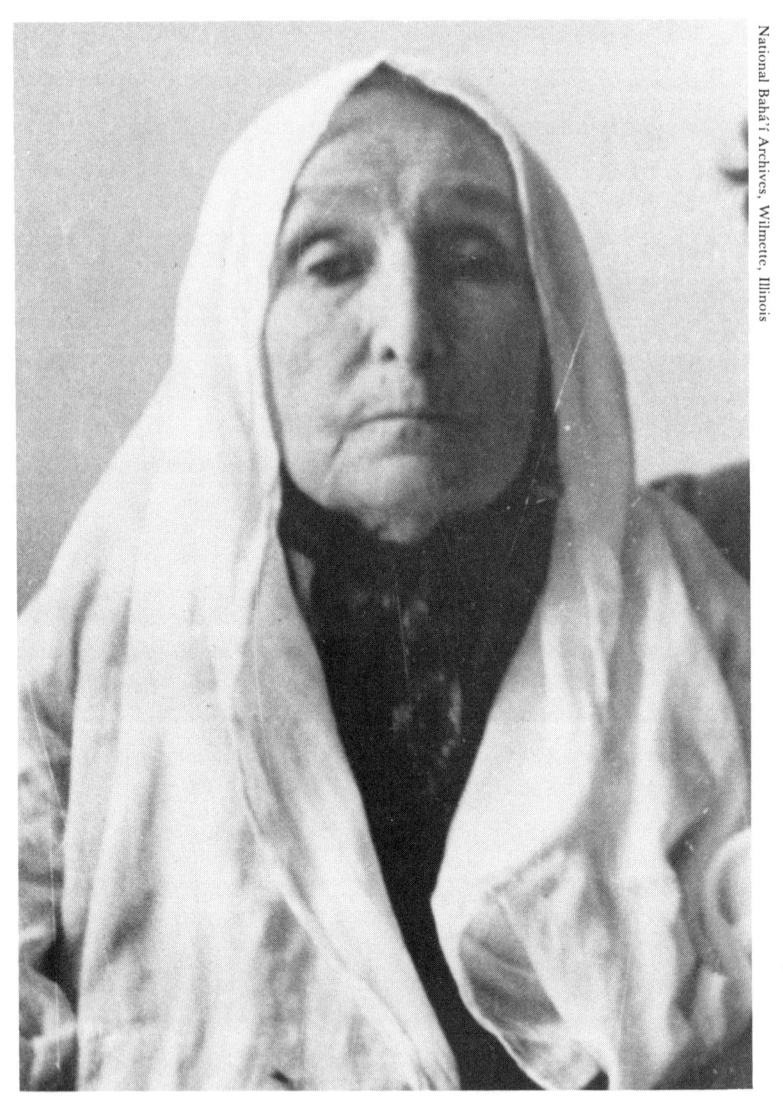

National Bahá'í Archives, Wilmette, Illinois

MUNÍRIH KHÁNUM
in later years.

Letter of Lament: 1922

O my Lord, O my Lord. Forsake me not, for troubles have encompassed me on all sides. Lord! Lord! leave me not to myself, for misfortunes have seized me and assailed me.

O Peerless One! O Beloved One! O 'Abdu'l-Bahá! O tender and faithful Master! It is today one full year since You disappeared from our sight and winged Your flight to the Abhá Kingdom.* In that most glorious paradise, that supreme dwelling, You have chosen to make Your asylum and refuge, in perfect peace and comfort. O kind and loving Master: for fifty years You fed us from the breast of mercy. At every morn You would call all to gather, and You would even instruct us to "wake the small children and, after breakfast, read the prayers and Tablets." Cast Your glance of favor upon this poor, sorrow-stricken family from that other world, from the

*'Abdu'l-Bahá passed away at about 1:00 A.M., on November 28, 1921.

Sadratu'l-Muntahá.* Look down upon these leaves scattered in many lands and regions. Each one is in a different place and subjected to severe afflictions.

Should I wish to describe fully this miserable year, and that midnight thunderbolt, I would need seventy reams of paper, and seas of blood would pour from all eyes.

O Bahá, Knower of our inmost thoughts,
Thou seest the fire in our souls.
Yet, Thou inquirest not, Thou Self-Subsisting,
After the nightingales so lovingly nurtured by Thee.
My home is in ruins, its foundations destroyed;
I am caught in the talons of the eagle of sorrow.
Call me to that other land, by Thy leave,
To build my home in another nest, another tree.
This wide world, this limitless space
without Thee, Beloved One, encages me.
Turn our night into day, O Generous One;
Grant us wings to soar towards Thee.
Bestow upon Haifa a new creation,
Whose eyes will never gaze upon the likes of Thee,
Or behold Thy exalted stature,
Or those life-giving smiles of Thine.

Lord, Lord, Thou seest and knowest that these grieving hearts have lost all patience and strength. The thin

*The tree beyond which there is no passing. Here a reference to paradise.

thread of endurance is breaking. Resolution and tenacity have come to an end. The absence of the Most Excellent Branch [Shoghi Effendi],* and the lack of any news from Him have completely sapped the strength of the Greatest Holy Leaf [Bahíyyih Khánum], and of Rúḥá, the Holy Leaf ['Abdu'l-Bahá's daughter]. No longer is there vigor or strength or forebearance.

My own sorrows are beyond description. Each of the Holy Leaves is in a different town or region, dejected and helpless. Their houses are empty. All are witness to their absence. Jacob lost but one son, and that separation turned him blind. What am I to do, for I have lost a world of fathers? Well may You imagine how life is for this weak and infirm woman. It is beyond description.

I implore and supplicate at the Threshold of Oneness that You extend the Hand of Power and raise the bright moon of the Most Excellent Branch above the horizon of Haifa; that the Holy Leaves return in good health to the environs of the Abode of Light and the Supreme

*After the passing of 'Abdu'l-Bahá and his appointment as Guardian of the Bahá'í Faith, Shoghi Effendi found it necessary, because of his own deep grief and because of the troubles created by the enemies of the Cause, to leave the Holy Land for long periods. He entrusted the affairs of the Faith during these times to the supervision of the Greatest Holy Leaf. See *Bahá'í Administration* (Wilmette, Ill., 1928) p. 25; *The Priceless Pearl* (Oxford, 1969) pp. 56–77.

Dwelling Place*; and I ask that the promises made by 'Abdu'l-Bahá come about, so that the eyes of all the friends may be brightened and the hearts of all the Bahá'ís may become as rose-gardens. This is not beyond the power of God.

This maidservant entreats the devoted believers in the Ancient Beauty, and the near ones at the Threshold of the Greatest Name, to recite the Tablet of Aḥmad in these calamitous days, with complete concentration and in utter supplication, at the Shrines of Bahá'u'lláh and the Báb. God willing, this storm of sorrows will abate a little, this buffeted ship will reach the shore, and the light of the morn of hope will dawn.

That pure and holy, divine, benign, and benevolent Soul could never accept to see even one person sorrowful, and He did not wish that anyone should grieve. He would say, "I cannot bear to look upon a sorrowful face." He was the fellow-sufferer of all humanity and was loving to all on earth. When He spoke, it was usually with smiles and happiness. He would inquire after children. He desired that all should be cheerful and joyous. He would say, "Children are the inhabitants of the Kingdom. They are always happy and cheerful." . . .

But I must not pierce the hearts of the devoted ones any longer, or rub salt into the wounds of the sorrowing.

*The Shrine of Bahá'u'lláh and the Shrine of the Báb, respectively.

O our Lord, do not inflict upon us that which we cannot bear. Have mercy upon us through Thy generosity and bounty. Verily, Thou art the Forgiving, the All-Merciful, the Beneficent.

After this anguished account, it is my duty to offer my sincere thanks to all the Bahá'ís in every country and city and in all places. In truth, were it not for news of the steadfastness, fortitude, faithfulness, and lofty aspirations of the believers and handmaidens of the All-Merciful reaching us continuously by mail, by now the bonds of our existence would have been severed. That which has healed and consoled the wounded hearts of the Greatest Holy Leaf and these servants is this correspondence from afar, receiving news of the elevation of the Cause of God. There is not a shadow of a doubt that this news is a cause of joy to the heart of our Beloved in the Abhá Kingdom. It is for this reason that again I thank all, and I am profoundly grateful to all, from the bottom of my heart.

The handmaiden of
His Threshold,
Munírih

National Bahá'í Archives, Wilmette, Illinois

MUNÍRIH <u>KH</u>ÁNUM

Letter of Lament: 1923

O my Beloved, my Lord, and my Master. On this great night Your holy Soul is a witness from the Abhá Kingdom to my afflicted state and my wounded and inconsolable heart. O Solace of hearts, O Soother of souls, O Consoler of minds, and O ‘Abdu’l-Bahá! It is unbelievable that two years have passed since the radiant sun of your Beauty set, and that this weary one, this infirm one, this feeble one should remain in this painful prison-world. I have survived the days of separation and am still alive. I never imagined that I would go on this long.

O Envoy of the Blessed Beauty [i.e., Bahá’u’lláh]! O Thou who sitteth at the right hand of the Supreme Lord [i.e., the Báb]! What wrong was done that You suddenly turned Your favor away from us and hastened to that holy and radiant Kingdom? What happened that You wrote the first page of separation, and brought to an end the book of nearness. That You left behind the Greatest Holy Leaf; and the blessed fruits of the Most Glorious Tree; and the sorrowing and helpless Leaves; and the faithful believers—all willing to sacrifice their lives, with their hearts in shreds, run through by the arrow of fate. No physician can heal this; no remedy can be found, except for the bounty and favors of that generous, compassionate and loving Father, the Healer of all hopeless ills.

Alas! alas! O my Master and the Guide of every helpless one! What a disaster! What an earthquake at that midnight hour, that shattered a myriad powerful bonds with but one jolt. Whereupon cries and lamentation reached the heights of heaven, and anguish, agitation, and sorrow spread throughout the world of being.

Your distinguished Branch [Shoghi Effendi] in this long period did not seek intimacy or friendship with anybody, whether friend or stranger. He did not rest for even a moment, for he wandered continually across mountains and seas and wilderness, always alone and distant. But the bonds of His authority were strongly connected with the people of Bahá, and the cord of his loving kindness sublime and expansive in the land of the soul.

No one would have imagined or believed that, praise be to God, such steadfastness, perseverance, faithfulness, and sacrifice could be shown by the Bahá'ís during this period; or that, in spite of all the distress, and the absence of the Guardian of the Cause of God, the affairs of the Faith should proceed so smoothly and systematically, so efficiently and without interruption. Glad-tidings and good news reach here continuously from all places. In these lands whoever inquires about the Bahá'í Faith receives a reply without any fear or dissimulation. Indeed, in the newspaper *Mu'ayyad* it was reported that the Bahá'ís have requested the government to interview them so that "we can demonstrate the proofs of the Bahá'í Faith and our moral opinions."

That which is incumbent in this day on these servants and all Bahá'ís, and which is our duty after turning to the Guardian of the Cause, is to show strength and fortitude, faith, detachment, unity, and harmony, as well as a good character and other laudable qualities. We must be kind to all on earth and have goodwill toward all people, so that the radiance of this Most Great Cause will presently illumine and brighten the world of existence. It is hoped that humanity will be honored and ennobled by these praiseworthy virtues, and will follow the path of servitude. Clinging to the hem of the garment of grandeur, we will shed tears of repentance, and confess our helplessness and submission, saying:

"O unseen, but ever-present One! Assist and favor us in whatever manner is agreeable and acceptable to You. Make all the souls the dawningplaces of light; cultivate and make verdant the saplings of Your garden. Make of Your afflicted and fallen lovers guiding stars. Bestow upon Your servants of old a new light, so that we can act according to Your holy will, and by this the soul of the Blessed One can be contented and pleased with everyone. Indeed, there can be no greater joy or delight than the fulfillment of these wishes for these servants, who expect no rest or comfort on this earth. O Lord, aid us to do that which you desire and please. You are powerful over all, and benevolent and Merciful unto all Your servants."

On this auspicious night, O Lord of past and present,
O kind God, King of Grace and Bounty;
Scatter drops from the Sea of Bounty on these sorrowing hearts,
Give me life anew in this existence.
Save You, O King of Justice, who do your servants have?
But for you, Companion in our sorrows, who do we have?

I beg all for their kind prayers and supplications for assistance.

Munírih

MUNÍRIH KHÁNUM (l.) WITH THE GREATEST HOLY LEAF

Letter of Lament: 1933

O my Lord, O my Lord. Forsake me not, for troubles have encompassed me on all sides. Lord, Lord, leave me not to myself, for misfortune has assailed and seized me.

I sit to write a fitting letter:
  A letter of swelling sorrow;
Soiled with my heart's blood,
  Patterned with my tears;
Black as Layli's tresses,
  Laid waste like Majnun's soul;
Lacerated like a lover's heart,
  Grieved from first to last.
O Believers! Immersed in my sorrow and woe
  I raise the cup of my own blood to my lips.
Should I say more, breasts would pound.
  Should I write all, hearts would break.
Whither my Companion, Friend of my soul,
  That gentle Confidant of my secret thoughts?
Would that my tears become the sea,
  Where I might cast my sorrows.
O woe, O woe, O woe is me,
  That our precious Sun should be veiled
    by a cloud.

O remembrance of the Blessed Beauty, O sister of 'Abdu'l-Bahá, O Greatest Holy Leaf! You have melted us in the furnace of separation and remoteness. You have ascended to your eternal nest in the Kingdom of Abhá.* You have even caused the Most Excellent Branch to be depressed and downcast in the prime of his youth and vigor. Now he seeks the company of no one, and is neither happy nor cheerful.

You have cast your Brother's dear children in the fire of separation. They seek neither the company of friend nor of stranger. They sorrow and mourn at all times, and their tears are always flowing.

O friend of our spirits, and solace of our lives, was it not enough for us to have the calamity of the setting of the Most Great Luminary, the Guide of the peoples of the world, Bahá'u'lláh?—May my soul, my being, my existence be a sacrifice for His Name.

Was it not enough for us to bear that sudden blow, the midnight flight, of the Most Great Branch ['Abdu'l-Bahá]? That was cause for cries of grief and lament from the people of Palestine to reach the heights of heaven, and for all means of pleasure to be abandoned. Indeed, joy and entertainment are so foreign to us that when the merest mention of these is made, our Bahá'í youth immediately ask that "such things not be spoken of in front

*Bahíyyih Khánum, the Greatest Holy Leaf, passed away on July 15, 1932.

Bahá'í World Center

THE GREATEST HOLY LEAF
Bahíyyih Khánum, as a young woman.

of us, for we are weary of the world and all its pleasures." Then they withdraw from us.

As for myself, I have found no solution other than to come to this radiant and sacred spot, the resting place of the Greatest Holy Leaf, which faces that Most Glorious Resting Place, and also the Shrines of the Báb and 'Abdu'l-Bahá. Here I make my home and seek refuge, and pray to the court of the Judge of all our needs.

O our Lord, O our Lord, depart not from our hearts, since Thou hast guided us and granted us compassion from Thy presence. Verily Thou art the Giver.

O my Beloved, "better that I break away from all things and turn instead to Thy Court" for as He has said: "*Wouldst thou have Me, seek none other than Me; and wouldst thou gaze upon My beauty, close thine eyes to the world and all that is therein.*"*

And now, O Mistress of the World and of the handmaids of the All-Merciful: today is one whole year since you winged your flight from this world of sorrow and pain, and made your home and refuge in the Abhá Kingdom, and in the supreme paradise. O, that I could be with you! What triumph that would be for me!

The faithful maidservant of the
Most-Sacred Threshold,
Munírih

*The Hidden Words, Persian, No. 31.

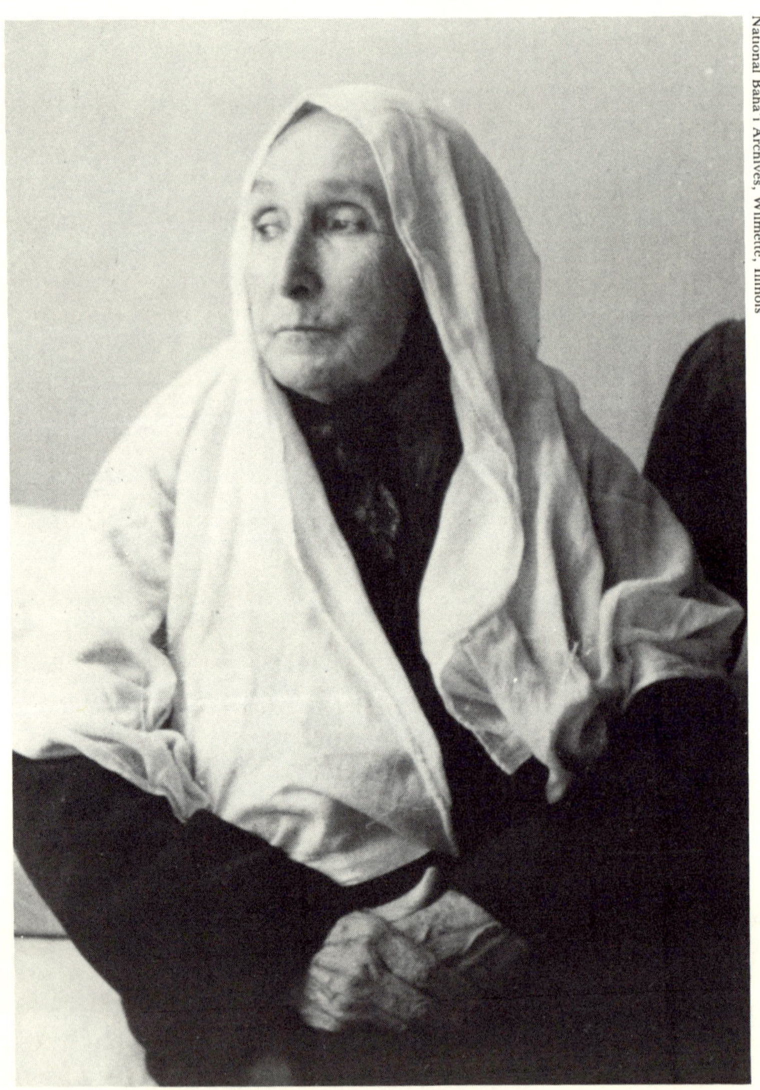

National Bahá'í Archives, Wilmette, Illinois

MUNÍRIH KHÁNUM

Letter of Lament

[date unknown]

O my Beloved, O Bahá'u'lláh! Your holy and blessed Being bears witness to what befell the members of the Holy Household and Your near ones after Your ascension as a result of internal conflicts in the Cause of God.

That Blessed Branch did not pass one peaceful night; that Greatest Holy Leaf never saw her incomparable Brother happy or joyful; and this afflicted handmaiden spent most of her time weeping, praying, and reciting laments, reading the *Muṣíbat Námih*,* and other heart-rending poems. I can endure no more. My patience is ended. My powers have declined. I live on Mount Carmel friendless and alone.

O 'Abdu'l-Bahá, I cry out at my remoteness from Thee;
O 'Abdu'l-Bahá, I commit myself to Thy care.

I have no desire to return to my home. I do not know what to do. It is befitting that I end with the words of Ṭáhirih, O my Master.

*Title of a work by the Persian poet 'Attár.

Thy radiant face,
Thy shimmering hair,
Compel me to Thee,
Hastily, eagerly.

O answerer of the needy!

The handmaiden of the
Sacred Threshold,
Munírih

Note: Munírih Khánum passed away on 30 April, 1938. For tributes and recollections, see *The Bahá'í World* (Wilmette, Ill., 1942) vol. VIII (1938–1940) pp. 260–267.

Letter: The Girls School Project

To the loved ones of God and handmaids of the Merciful: upon them all be the Glory of God, the Most Glorious.

It is clear and evident that the edifice of existence is founded upon education. That is, were it not for training, no created thing could exist, and nothing would achieve life or vitality.

In this most bountiful age, this most fair and splendid century, the Ancient Beauty—exalted be His Most Great Name—has ranked education among the most important matters, in the forefront of His divine and excellent commandments. He has explicitly and decisively laid stress upon this important issue. On numerous occasions and in countless places He has urged and exhorted fathers and mothers; the peoples of the world; people of goodwill in all lands and nations; indeed, even the kings and rulers of the world, and those endowed with honor and lofty ideals, to carry out this illustrious work, which is considered among the most excellent of works in the sight of God, as recorded and confirmed in the inmost hearts of the divine Tablets and in the Sacred Texts.

During the day of the Covenant of 'Abdu'l-Bahá, may our souls be a sacrifice at His Most Pure Threshold, He emphasized this matter of education. He has declared it to be among the greatest of the divine precepts, and accounted its acquisition as an imperative necessity. He has praised and favored those who have arisen to render this great service. He warned of the loss of the pleasure of the True One should there be any negligence, heedlessness, or laxness in the execution of this critical injunction.

Indeed, the writings of the Pen of the Covenant overflow with this theme, placing particular emphasis on the instruction and refinement of girls. He has attested and explained that as the girls of today will be the mothers of tomorrow, then it is obvious that a child's first educator is the mother. If a mother is not adorned as she should be with heavenly behavior and endowed with spiritual qualities, and if she has not acquired humane virtues and morals, then of course she will be remiss in her duty of instructing and refining her children, and imperfections and defects will result. For "how can lifeless matter be the bearer of a vital spark?"

Thus the education of girls is a matter of the greatest importance and is regarded as an obligatory law. Hence, the friends of the All-Merciful, and the beloved maidservants of the Lord, in all cities and countries must take action and endeavor to their utmost capacity to carry out this weighty injunction.

Be that as it may. Praise be to God, through the

bounty of the Blessed Beauty, there are girls schools in many places. They are already established and well-organized. It is strongly hoped that this will become a universal trend and will become more widespread.

From early on in my life, I always hoped and envisaged that the means for the progress and success of Bahá'í girls, and indeed, for the girls of all nations, would come about. And I hoped that, God willing, all would become intoxicated with the wine of the love of God, and all would attain to heavenly behavior and the knowledge of God. That their hearts, which are the dawning-places of the effulgences of divine bounties, would become paradises of Abhá; and that they would attain unto the reality of the most great gift of "*Ye are the fruits of one tree, and the leaves of one branch*," this being the most great beneficence and means of ennoblement. Then will service to the world of humanity reach its highest summit.

When I was in the presence of the Light of the Covenant, the Luminous Orb of the Universe, I said, "If it is acceptable to You, we should establish a small school in Haifa for the children of the believers, so that they can be trained from their earliest childhood in Bahá'í behavior and become informed of the history of the Faith."

'Abdu'l-Bahá pointed His finger toward Mount Carmel and said, "This lofty mountain will eventually be covered with schools, hospitals, and guest houses. The promises made by the Prophets will be realized and fulfilled."

Then I said, "I was thinking of Hájí Mírzá Ḥasan's land, on which several simple buildings could be built,"

But He replied: "No. All of the land opposite to the Shrine of the Báb, which is owned by Áqá 'Abbás 'Alí, a small piece of which was offered by him as a gift at Riḍván, and which We accepted, must be bought up. That is an excellent site for a school. It is spacious, the air is clean, and it is opposite the Shrine of the Báb."

At that time the faithful leaf and respected handmaid of God, Miss Sanderson (Rúḥíyyih), was present. She implored and supplicated 'Abdu'l-Bahá, saying, "I too would like to participate in this venture."

To which 'Abdu'l-Bahá replied: "Very well, it is accepted."

The revered Mr. Mason Remey—upon him be the Glory of God, the Most Glorious—drew the plans for the school, and they were shown to 'Abdu'l-Bahá.

The purpose in writing all this is to say that the land for the school is available. It consists of 12,000 *dhar'* in area. I have already contributed a trifling 1,500 lira. Another 1000 lira, or slightly less, has been donated by others. But it is obvious that this excellent and worthy task, requires the magnanimity of the believers, and needs the action of the friends. God willing, in the time of Most Excellent Branch—may the souls of all be a sacrifice to Him—together with the efforts of the Holy Leaves, and the aid and assistance of our devoted brothers and sisters, it will be carried out and completed.

O Lord, turn our hopes into reality so that our hearts

can rejoice. Bind us to your near servants and devoted handmaidens.

The handmaiden of the
Sacred Threshold,
Munírih

It should be noted that the method given by the Guardian of the Cause, Jináb-i Shoghi Effendi—may the souls of all be a sacrifice to Him—concerning this matter should be carried out to the letter. The method of payment for the school is that anyone sending a contribution should send it in the names of the Blessed Leaves, the daughters of ‘Abdu’l-Bahá—may our souls be a sacrifice at His noble and sanctified Threshold.

The receipts will also have to be signed by those four daughters, that is: Ḍiyá’íyyih Kh͟ánum, Ṭúbá Kh͟ánum, Rúḥá Kh͟ánum, and Munavvar Kh͟ánum. These will be sent to the contributors. The donations will be deposited in the bank in Haifa, in the account of the Blessed Leaves, until such a time when enough money has been collected.

Without a doubt, every beginning was initially but a modest one. Now we too must be content with starting in a small way.

Munírih

National Bahá'í Archives, Wilmette, Illinois

MUNÍRIH KHÁNUM

Letter: Service of Women to the Cause

May my life be a sacrifice for the leaves who are firm in the Covenant of God.

First of all, glad tidings; and above all, happiness; and most of all, delight at the arrival of the Most Excellent Branch in the Holy Land, to the Shrine of the Báb and the Abode of Light [the Shrine of Bahá'u'lláh]. All the Bahá'ís are rejoicing at His arrival. Secondly, the most glorious tidings, the supreme gift for our spiritual sisters, for the handmaids of the All-Merciful, and the divine friends is certainly the news of the health and well-being of that Leaf of the Sacred Tree of Abhá, the Greatest Holy Leaf. May our souls be a sacrifice for the sorrows she has suffered. She joins the Holy Leaves in sending her loftiest Bahá'í sentiments to all the handmaids in those regions.

By the Grace and Favor of God, in spite of the setting of the Sun of the Covenant and the Ascension of the Beloved of the Universe, there has been a constant stream of good news and soul-stirring reports concerning the aspirations and steadfastness of the friends, the establishment of assemblies of teaching (*mahấfil-i tablíq*), of service to humanity, and of love and unity within the Bahá'í community. As soon as these tidings reach the environs of the Shrines of Bahá'u'lláh and the Báb, they brighten our tearful eyes, and heal these broken and wounded hearts. Indeed, this is as it should be, for in His Will and Testament 'Abdu'l-Bahá places great emphasis on this matter, saying:

> It behooveth them [i.e., The Hands of the Cause, the friends, and loved ones] not to rest for a moment, neither to seek repose. They must disperse themselves in every land, pass by every clime and travel throughout all regions. Bestirred, without rest and steadfast to the end . . .

Thus, we must be comforted by the example of the disciples of Christ and observe how they behaved after His ascension. Mary Magdalene was but a village woman, but her star is still rising in the heavens of Christianity. And Ḥusníyyih was but a slave girl of the Household of Muḥammad. On several occasions she debated with the caliphs, proving to them the truth of the people of the House of 'Alí [the Shí'ís]. Her name is still recorded in the books of Shí'ih Islam, and her place is assured in the dispensation of Muḥammad. And Ṭáhirih—may my soul be a sacrifice for her, although her days of service and sacrifice were not many, yet in the heaven of the Cause of God she became a brilliant star and a heavenly luminary. Now the believers of both the East and the West and the handmaidens in America adorn every occasion with the name of Ṭáhirih. This is because among the men there were numerous steadfast and devoted believers who gave their pure lives in the field of sacrifice, but among women these have been few and far between.

By the grace and favor of God, 'Abdu'l-Bahá has elevated the station of women in this radiant age. He has altered the quranic verse: "Men are the custodians of women." He has taught that men and women are like the two wings of a bird, and neither is superior to the other. Girls should be educated in the same way as boys, perhaps even given preference.

Bahá'u'lláh has said that in this age, leaves [i.e., women] will appear who will become the glory of the men of the world.

Without a doubt the promises of God will come about and will be manifested soon. We have heard that nowadays in Tehran, fifty women have offered their enthusiastic services in any capacity. This news has made these servants very, very happy. I have asked for the names of each of those dear sisters, so that I can write to each one and let her know that the mention of her service has been made and is known in the Holy Land.

And so, my dear and respected sisters, thanks be to God that the field of service in the Cause of God is extensive and souls with capacity are ready. Seekers and thirsty ones are waiting, and those leaves are prepared and willing to sacrifice. Yet, how regretable it is that some of the people of Iran are still bloodthirsty, cruel, and merciless. "Alas, no time is there to contemplate the beauteous garden of the lovers of the Age."

News has reached us that two revered maidservants have set out to teach the Faith. One is the daughter of the late minister Muḥtaram Íṣfahání, and the other is the sister of the twin shining lights.* We were cheered and delighted by this news. The accounts of gatherings in Qazvin, and also in America, have brought us a world of happiness.

It is clear and evident that today the hope and aspiration of all the believers is to see the elevation of the Cause of God. We supplicate and beseech at the Court of the Lord of Oneness that He shelter and defend all the friends in the sanctuary of His protection and care and aid them to perform services worthy of the Sacred Threshold.

But still, how grievous, how lamentable that we have been deprived of union with the Incomparable One. We are afflicted with eternal separation; the compassionate Beloved is hidden from our eyes, and that Sun of Bounty and Favor is concealed in the Place of Reunion. The Reason for joy remains hidden, and the Essence of rejoicing and gladness has chosen concealment. As He, Himself, has said: "*The time cometh, when the nightingale of holiness will no longer unfold the inner mysteries and ye will all*

*The King of Martyrs and the Beloved of Martyrs.

be bereft of the celestial melody and of the voice from on high."*
Alas, alas that it was decreed and has come to pass.

The triumphant day of God has come and gone, alas;
  The Sea of Bounty, the Waves of Favors,
    have ebbed and flowed, alas;
Lament for this loss, O Existence, this separation.
  O mourner, shed tears of blood.
Alas, alas, where has the King gone?
  O world, where the commander?
Where is the Knower of Divine Mysteries,
  the Diviner of Secrets?

All the paper in the universe, all the pens of the world, would be incapable of recording the tale of this separation. However, we must cling to the cord of patience and perseverance. No further will I wound the injured hearts of my spiritual sisters, nor recount the bitterness of separation from the Light of the Universe. Our hope is that in this coming year divine assistance and aid from on high will so surround the Bahá'ís that the splendors and effects thereof will be beyond description.

Verily, He is kind and compassionate unto His servants.

The maidservant of
Your Sacred Threshold,
Munírih

*The Hidden Words, Persian, No. 15.